The Baddest Kid
in
Kindergarten

DEDICATION

This book is dedicated to all the little children entering Kindergarten.

*Special thanks
to my friend and mentor
Sonica Ellis*

It was a warm spring day when Derek
and his mom took a trip
to the ice cream stand.

They walked hand in hand,
occasionally stopping to read
house numbers and count cars.

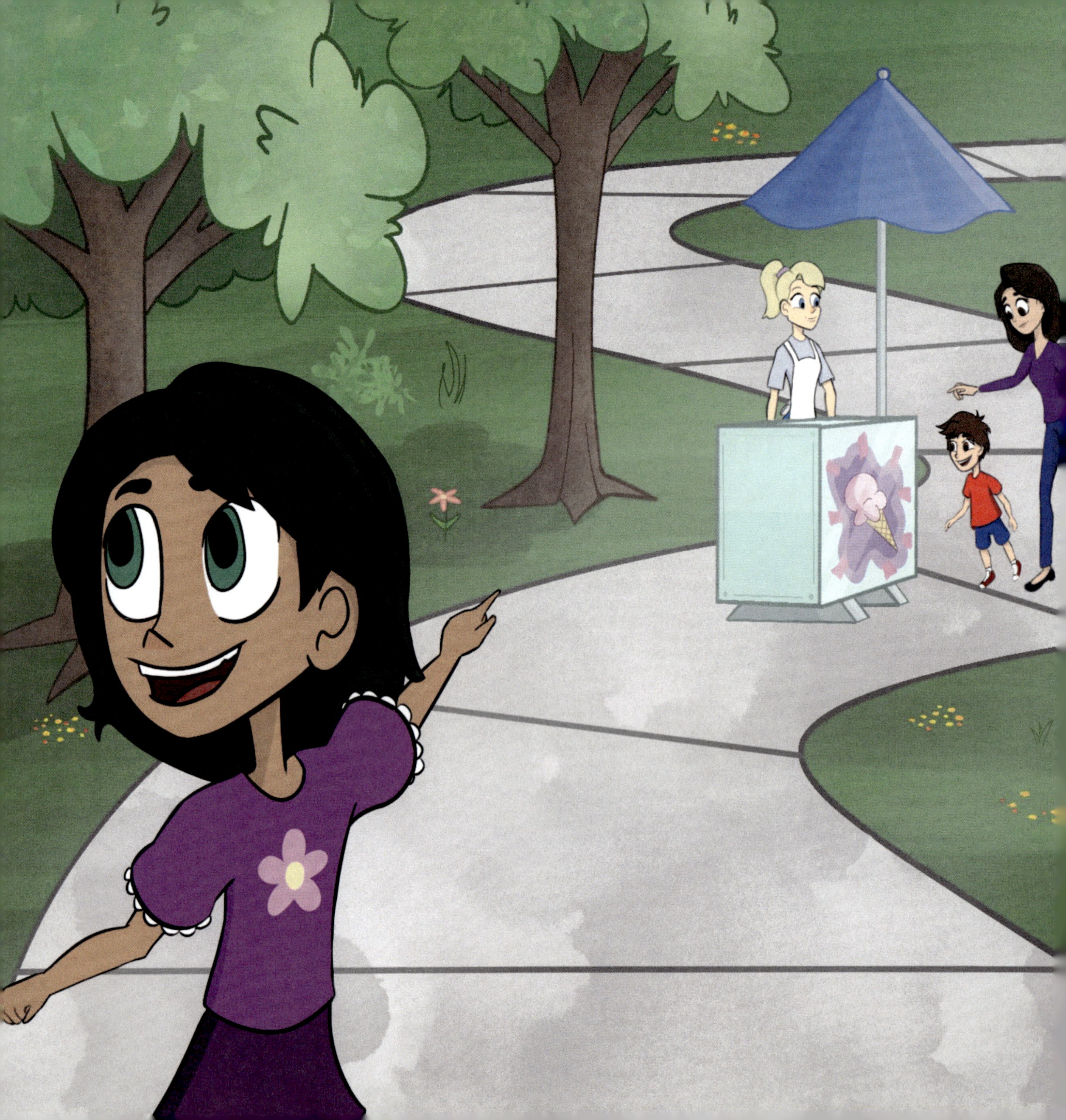

While they waited in line, Derek's classmate Lilly spotted him.

"Mom" she shouted, "That's Derek Palmer! He's the baddest kid in kindergarten."

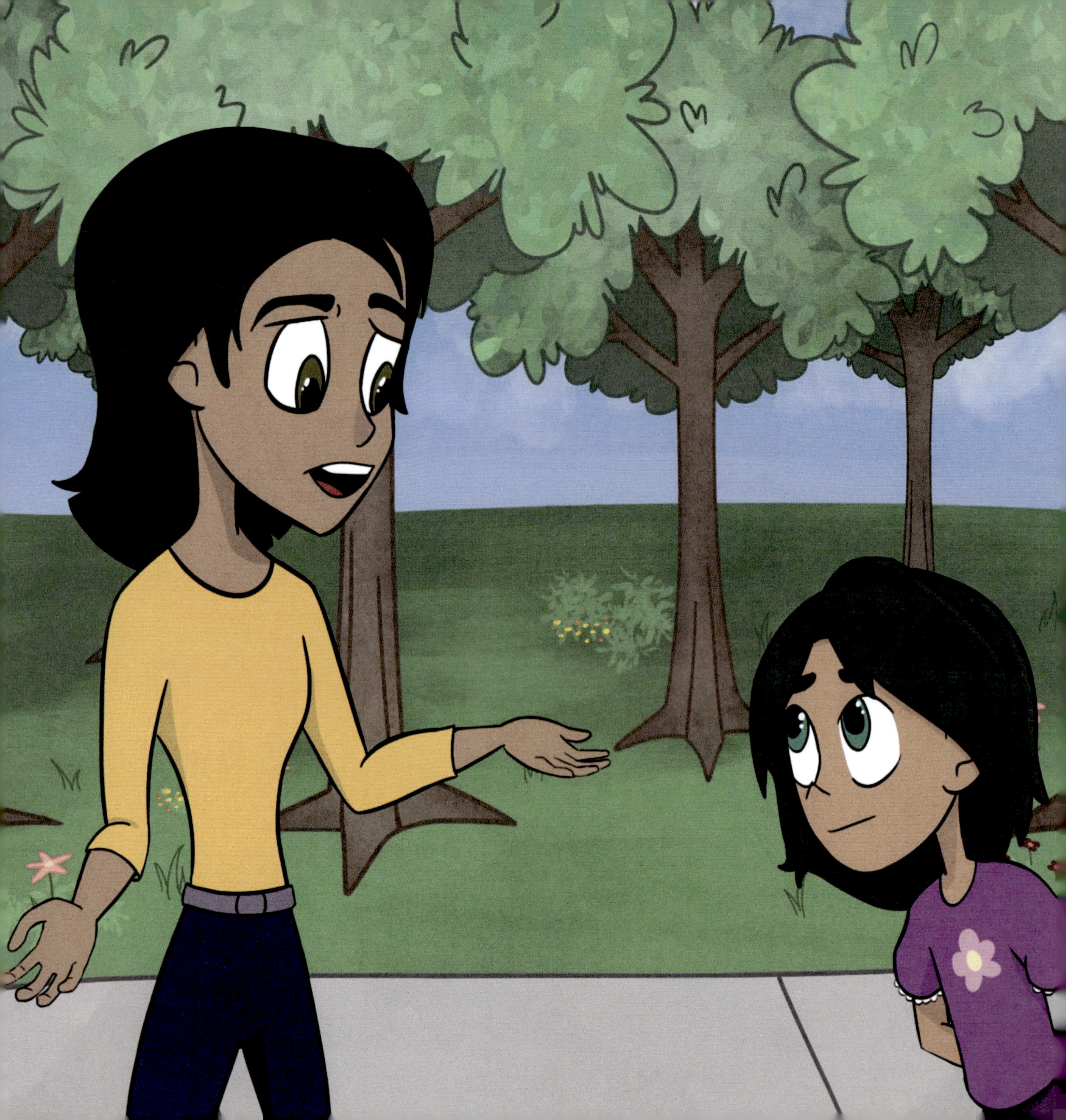

"Lilly!" Lilly's mother exclaimed, "That's not nice!"

"I'm sorry," said Lilly, a little embarrassed.

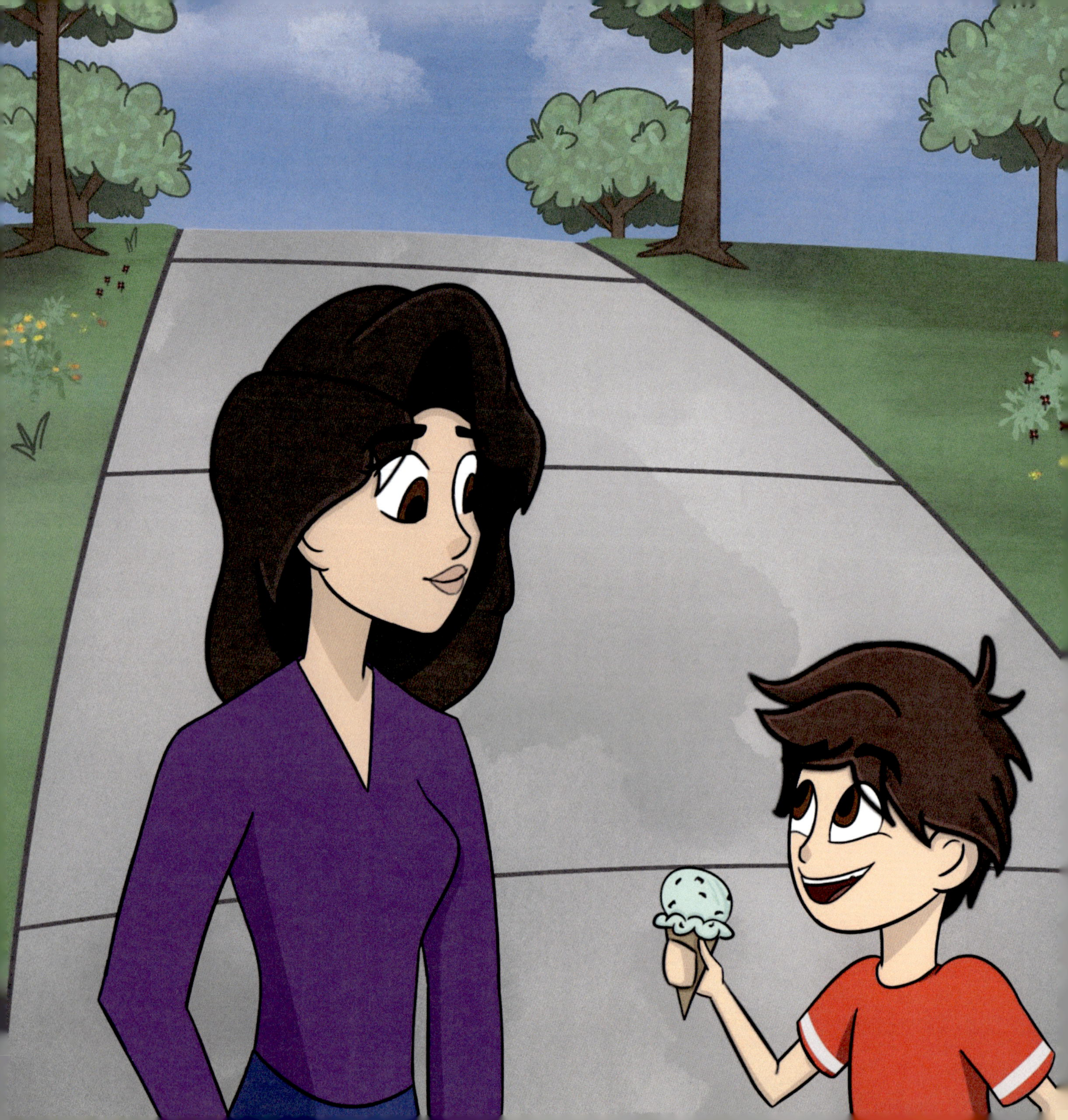

"That's ok" said Derek's mom,
"I know Derek can be a handful sometimes."

Derek and his mom got their ice cream and walked home, enjoying the warm sun.

Derek wasn't really bad.
He was just excited to go to school and he had lots of energy.

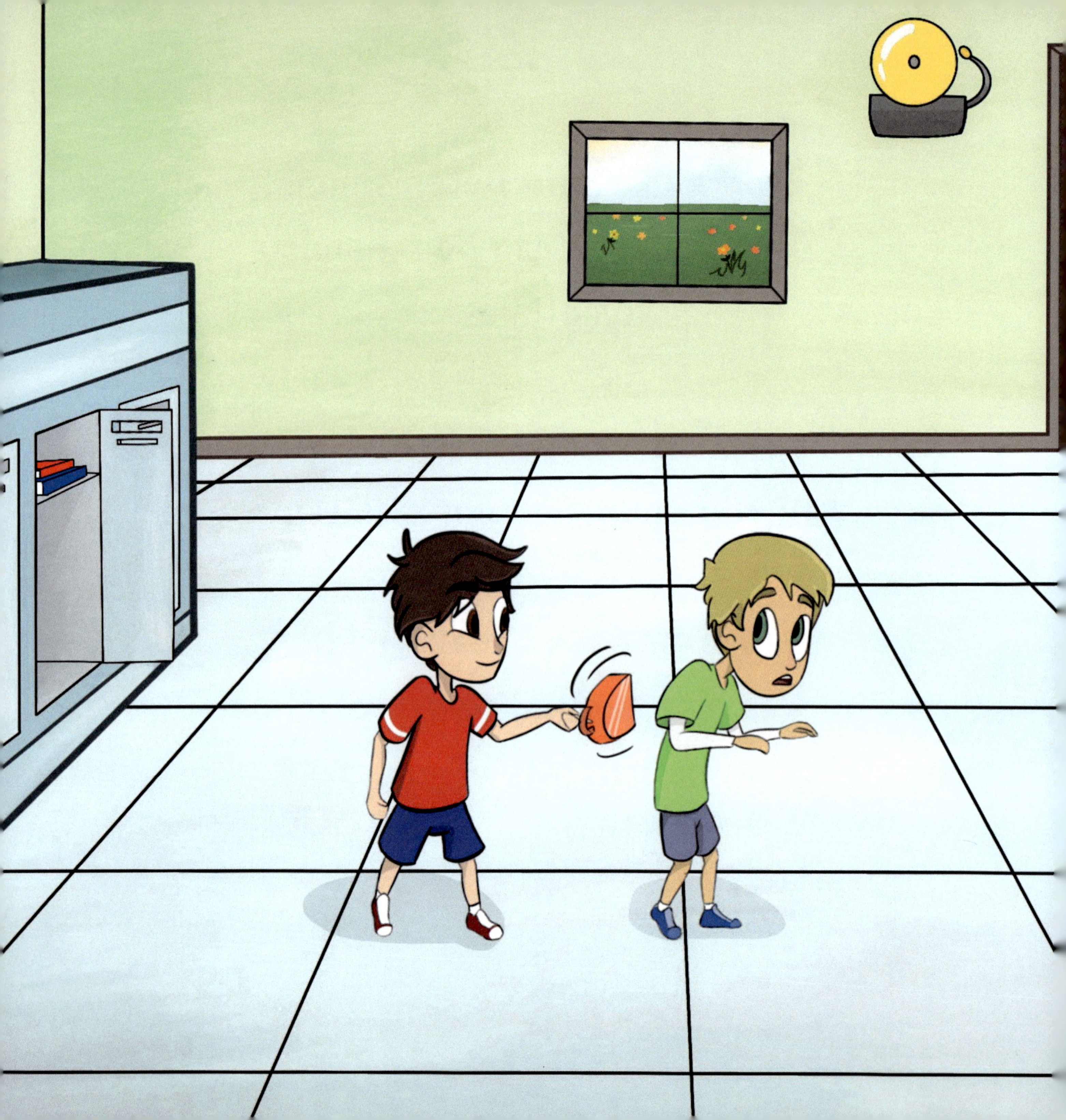

The next day at school Derek was
so excited for lunch that
he swung his lunchbox around
nearly hitting his friend!

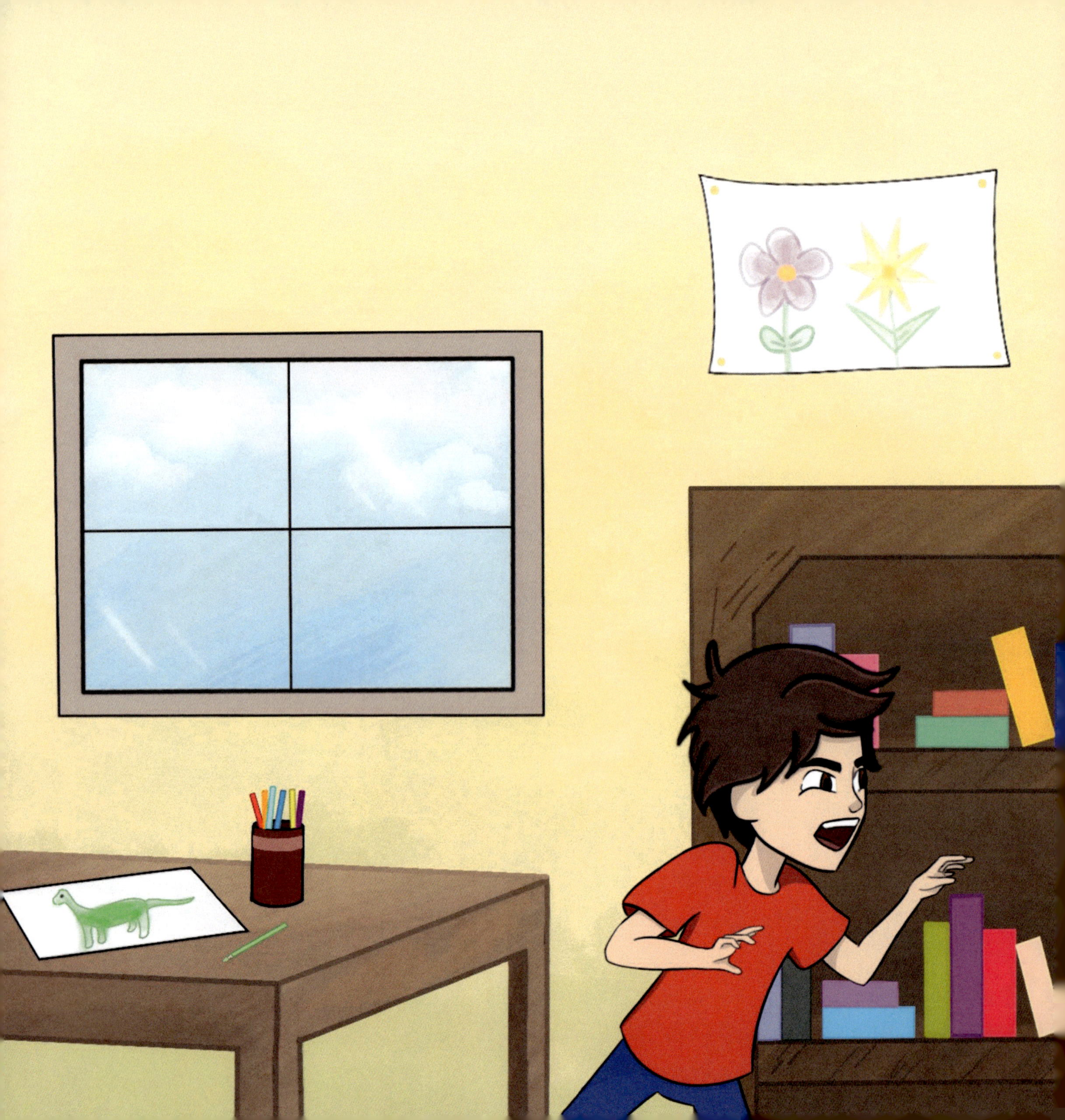

Later that day during "quiet time"
at the library, Derek hid under the table
and let out a big ROAR,
which startled his teacher so much
that she dropped the book she was reading.

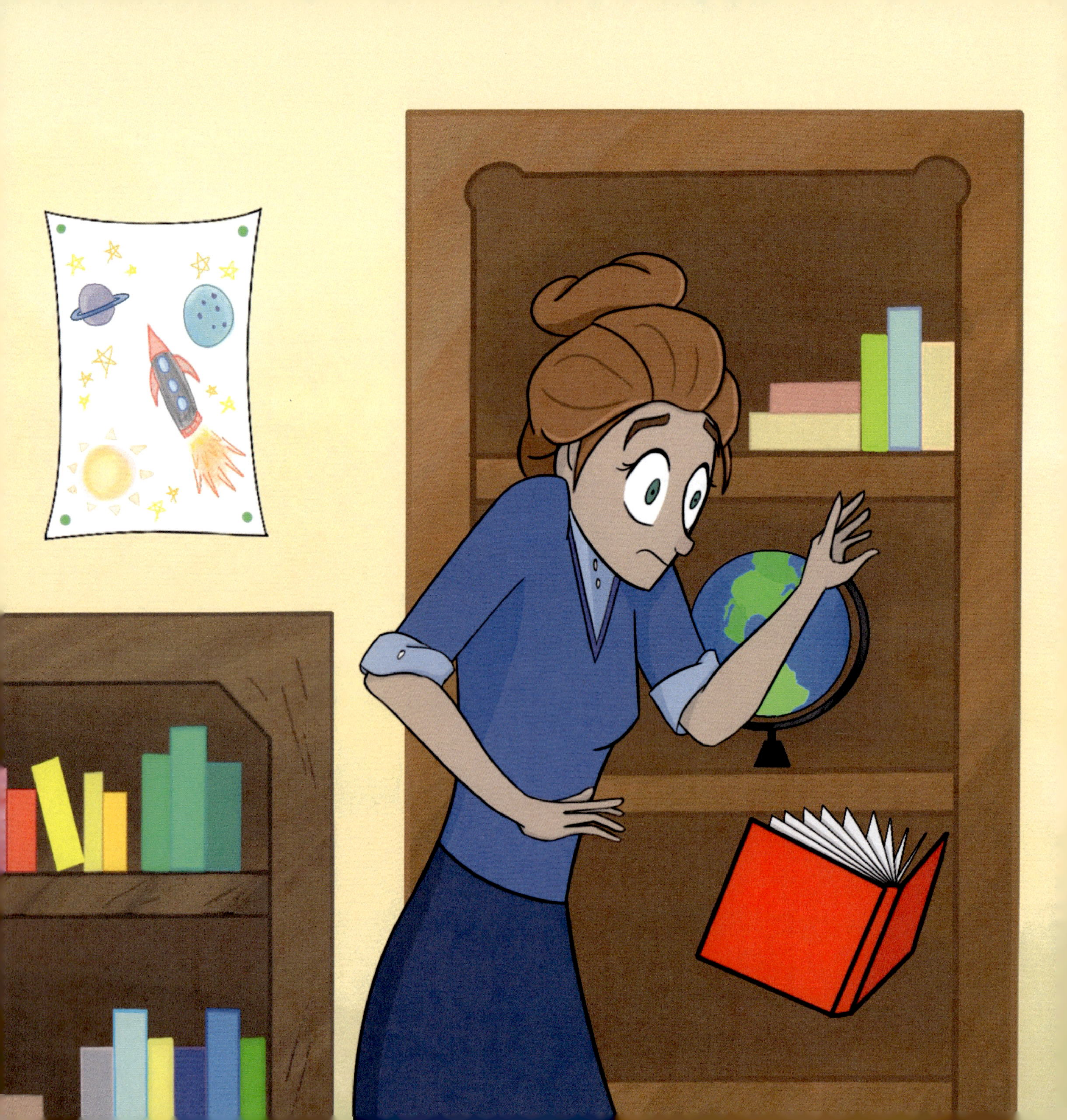

"Derek Palmer", the teacher said,
picking up her book,
"you need to be quiet.
Your friends are reading.
Inside voices only please."

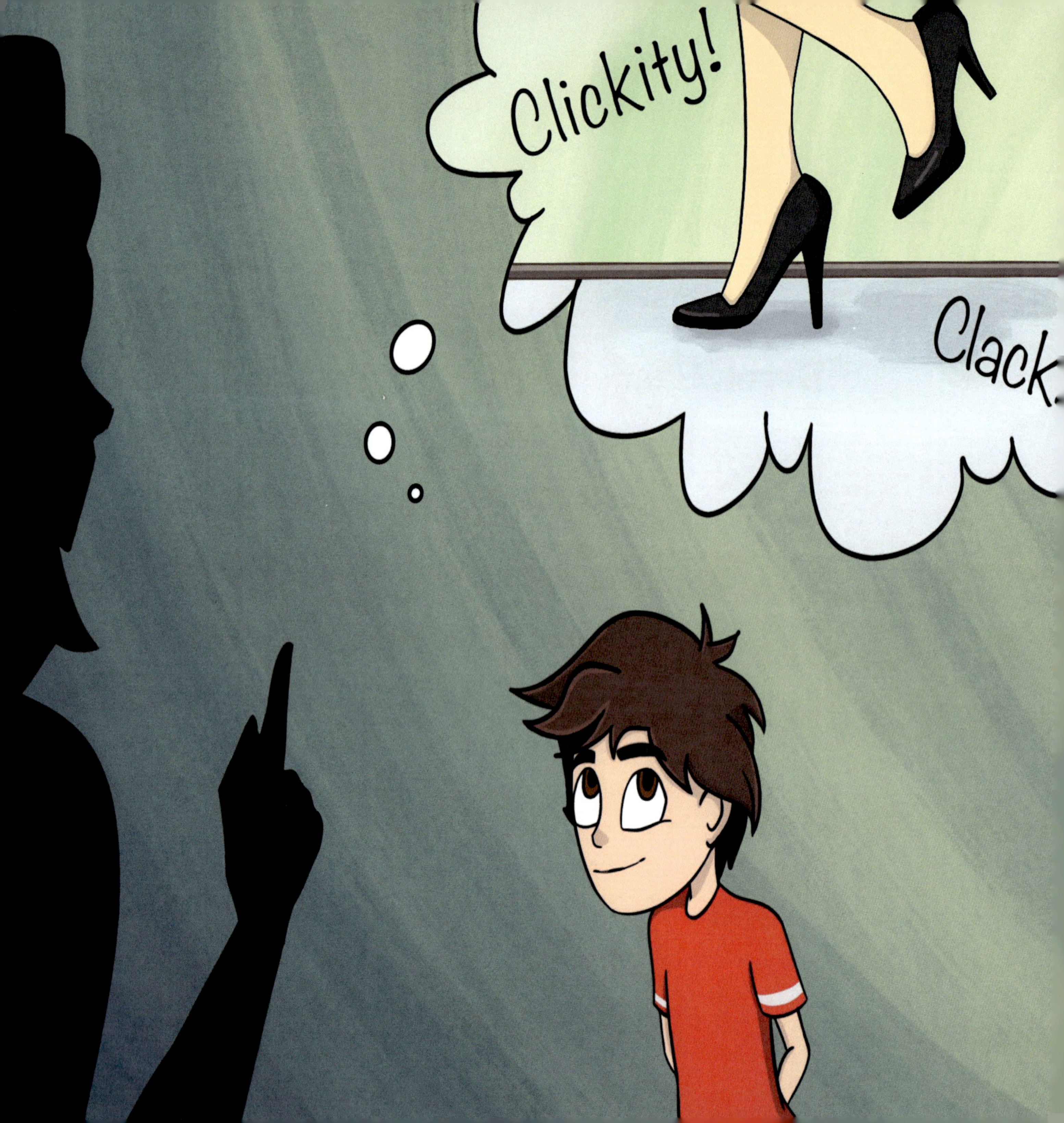
Clickity!
Clack.

When Derek got home that day,
his mom tried to talk to him
about how to behave in school,
but he wasn't really listening.

Instead he was telling his mother how
the teacher's heels went "clickity clack"
when she walked down the hallway.

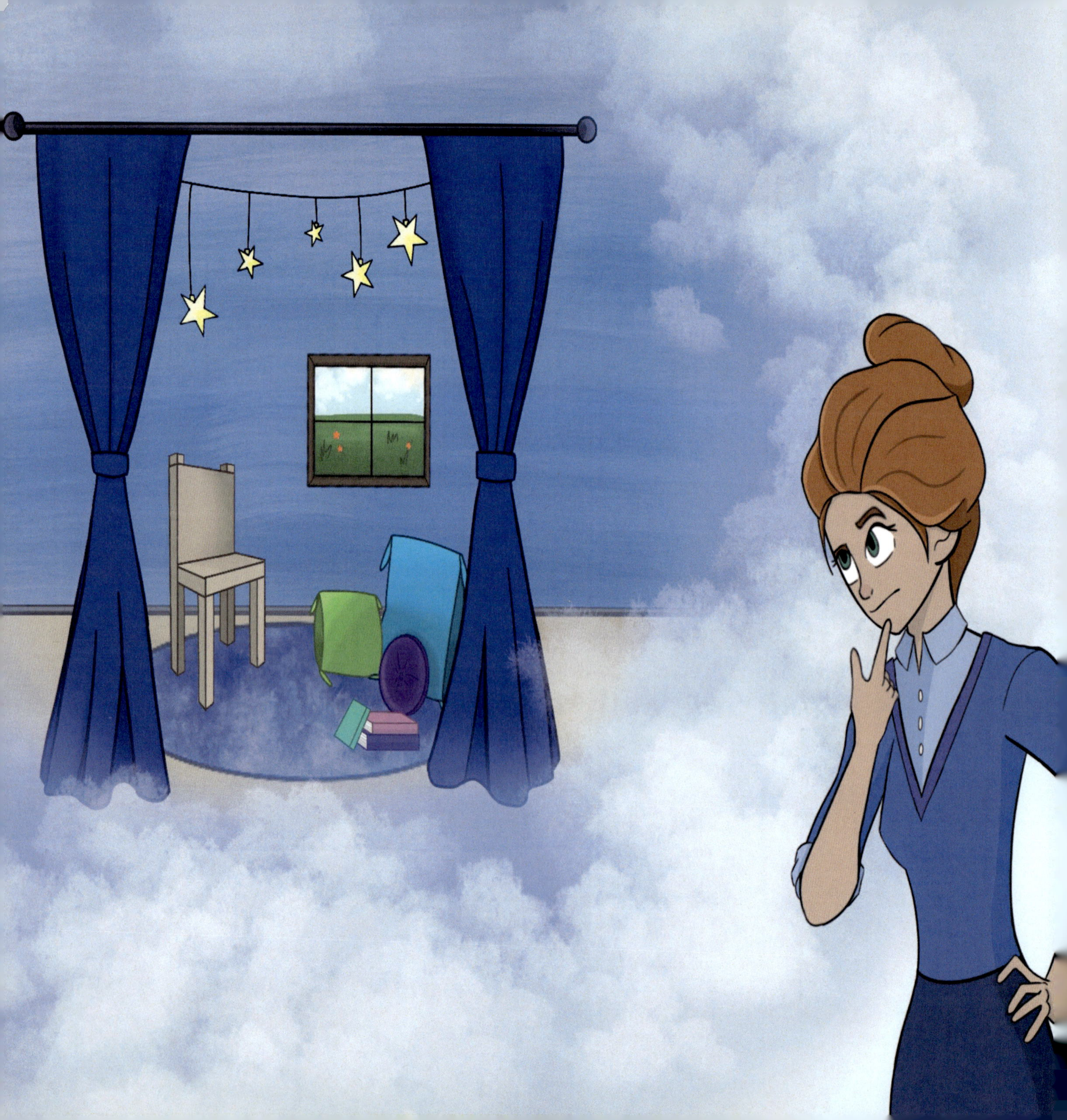

Derek's teacher thought and thought about how she could help Derek to be more successful in school.

Then she had an idea! She created a "quiet space" in her classroom. It had a rug, a beanbag chair, and plenty of books and puzzles.

She told Derek that if he was having trouble sitting still, he could go to the "quiet space" until he was ready to go back to his desk, ready to learn.

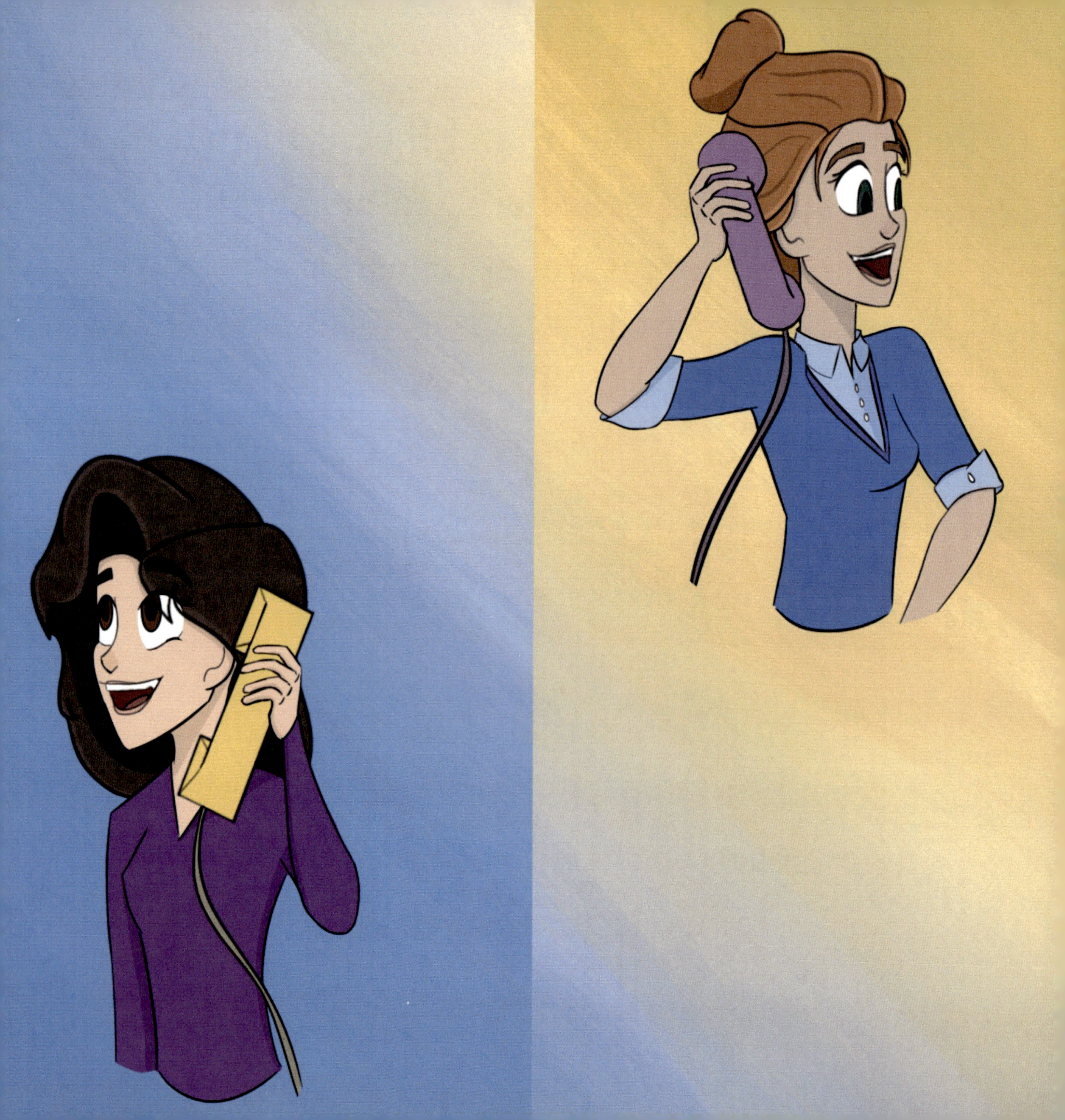

Everyday Derek's mother checked on his progress.

"How was Derek today?"

And more often than not,
the teacher gave her good news.

"Derek spent some time in the "quiet space"
and was well behaved and ready to learn
the rest of the day!"

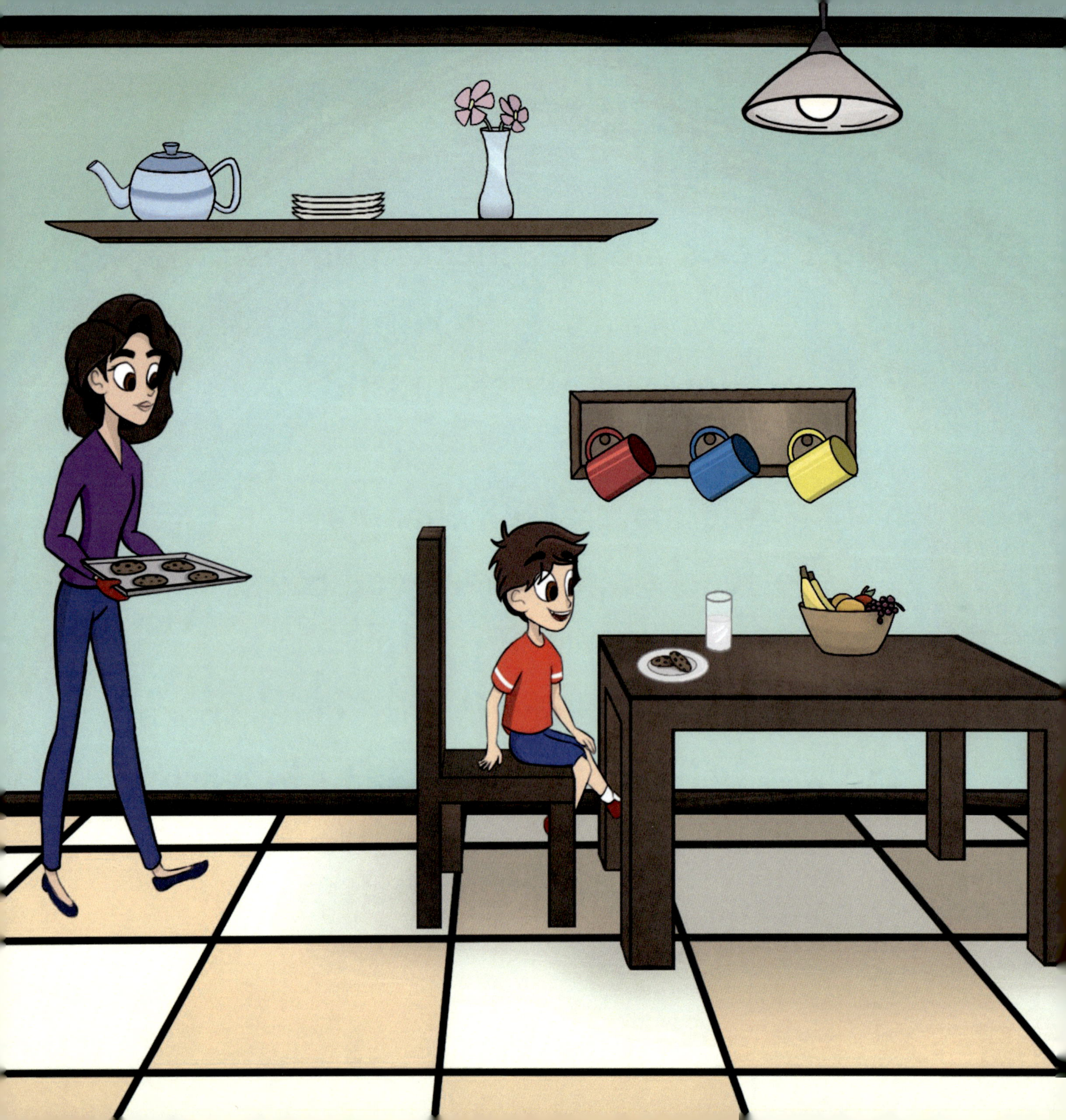

After a week of good reports,
Derek's mom had his favorite snack
waiting for him when
he got home from school.

You see, Derek was not really
the baddest kid in kindergarten.

In fact, he was not bad at all.
He just needed a little help.
Between Derek's teacher, the
"quiet space" and his mom's
encouragement, Derek was just fine!

Made in the USA
Middletown, DE
30 June 2022